**Comhairle Contae
Fhine Gall**
Fingal County
Council

Clár Éire Ildánach
*Creative Ireland
Programme*
2017–2022

Rinceoil Fingal would like to thank Creative Ireland Programme and Fingal Co. Council for sponsoring the production of this book which will be an invaluable resource for generations to come.

This publication is dedicated to Jimmy Archer and the late Lenny Martin
In recognition of their dedicated contribution to the community of Rush
Especially their commitment to Rinceoil Fingal

Meas Mór

ISBN: 979 877 762 1764

Illustrations: Assumpta Glynn

Cover Design: Laoise Nugent-Burke

Transcription: Aine O'Donnell

ACKNOWLEDGEMENTS

A project such as this one cannot be undertaken without the co-operation and goodwill from a wide selection of participants, contributors and co-ordinators. Although initiated and managed by the committee of Rinceoil Fingal, a large part of the project depended on the involvement of the community of Rush and the wider Fingal area.

We sincerely convey our thanks and appreciation to everyone who helped out despite the challenging Covid-19 restrictions making it very difficult to achieve results that otherwise would have been a routine task.

We wish to thank all Composers, Musicians and Singers, whose names are listed on a separate page, for their contributions of material and talent which comprises the backbone of Ceol an tSraidbhaile Ros Eó.

Huge praise and thanks to our production team of Chris Browne of Studio 44 recording studio, Laoise Nugent-Burke for graphic design and editing, Aine O'Donnell for transcription, Assumpta Glynn for original artwork throughout the book, Peter Davis for his original painting of Rush harbour and Tony Nugent for the cupla focal. To Kara Nugent Davis, Valerie Croghan, *Eithne O'Donnell, Ann Losty, Jimmy Archer, Dorothy Coffey, Katie Coffey and Frances Dennis for their organising, scheduling, co-ordinating and keeping this show on the road skills.

We are indebted to Alice O'Reilly of Rush Library, Karen DeLacey of Fingal Archives, Patricia Matthews and Rory O'Byrne of Fingal Arts Office and The Creative Ireland Fund, for their co-operation, sponsorship and advice along the way.

Our grateful appreciation goes to The Irish Traditional Music Archives (ITMA) for their support and generosity in hosting the recordings on their website.

We extend our thanks to the families of Lenny Martin, Tommy Walsh and Chris Langan for their generosity in sharing photos and compositions of their loved ones. Thanks to Ned Wall, Carl Jones, Leo Bissett, Orlaith O'Donnell and Mary Maxwell for sharing their art and photographs.

To the community of Rush for their support and participation we thank you all.

RINCEOIL FINGAL

Annmarie Losty *(Chairperson)*

This book would not have been possible without the dedication, hard work and vision of Eithne O'Donnell our vice chairperson. Originally a Weldon, Eithne comes from a long line of talented musicians.

RÉAMHRÁ

Le beagnach tríocha bliain ar an gclog, sheol Rinceoil Fingal Tionscadal Ceoil Traidisiúnta Éireannach pobail le cabhair ó Chomhairle Contae Fhine Gall, trína Ciste Éire Ildánach. Tá meascán d'fhoinn agus amhráin traidisiúnta na hÉireann agus giotaí filíochta ann a cumadh go háitiúil agus a bhaineann go sonrach leis an Ros agus le muintir an Rois.

Tá an tionscadal seo ar an méar fhada le tamall anois ach le teacht Covid-19, lena dhianghlasálacha agus a shrianta, thug sé chun tosaigh é ar chlár oibre Rinceoil Fingal mar bhealach chun an pobal a choinneáil páirteach go cruthaitheach agus dírithe le linn na n-amanna aisteach seo.

Ba é an smaoineamh a bhí leis, an oiread ceoil, filíochta agus amhrán traidisiúnta arna gcumadh go háitiúil ó cheantar an Rois a bhailiú. Bheadh na píosaí seo caillte nó ní bheadh eolas ach ag fíorbheagán daoine orthu dá uireasa seo. Thug coiste Rinceoil Fingal faoin tasc. Rinneadh an bailiúchán seo a thaifeadadh, a thras-scríobh agus a fhoilsiú do na cartlanna áitiúla agus tá sé ar fáil ar fud chóras Leabharlann Fhine Gall ionas gur féidir le gach duine féachaint air, le nasc leis na taifeadtaí digiteacha arna óstáil ag ITMA (Taisce Cheol Dúchais Éireann). Sílim gur mar gheall ar an aer nó ar an uisce i gceantar an Rois a nocht an tionscadal seo méid ollmhór saothair iontach de chuid na mban, na bhfear agus na ndaoine óga áitiúla, ag cur iallach ar an gcoiste gan ach méid teoranta a roghnú mar nach raibh acu ach ciste teoranta le hoibriú leis. Anois agus é curtha i gcrích tabharfaidh sé deis do gach duine a bhfuil spéis acu ann tumadh isteach sa chorpas saothair seo agus na píosaí cumadóireachta breátha óna gcomhghleacaithe a bhlaiseadh. Is féidir leat bualadh isteach sa Leabharlann agus tuilleadh a fháil amach faoi d'oidhreacht cheoil áitiúil más amhrán dar teideal "Rachel the Ruby from Rush", cornphíopa "The Cairn at Knockabawn" nó ríl "The Old Mill Bar" atá uait.

Cibé rogha atá agat, tá rud éigin sa bhailiúchán seo do gach duine le taitneamh a bhaint as.

Jimmy Archer

Uachtarán, Rinceoil Fingal 2021

PREFACE

With almost thirty years on the clock, Rinceoil Fingal launched a community Traditional Irish Music Project with the help of Fingal County Council, through its Creative Ireland Fund. It features a mixed bag of locally composed traditional Irish tunes, songs and a bit of poetry that are specific to Rush and the people of Rush.

This project has been on the back burner for a while now but the arrival of Covid-19, with its lockdowns and restrictions, brought it to the forefront of Rinceoil Fingal's agenda as a way of keeping the community creatively involved and focused during these strange times.

The idea was to gather as much locally composed traditional Irish music, poems and songs from the Rush area that otherwise might be lost or known only to a few. The task was taken up by the committee of Rinceoil Fingal. This collection was recorded, transcribed and published for the local archives and is available throughout the Fingal Library system for all to peruse, with a link to the digital recordings hosted by the ITMA (Irish Traditional Music Archive). I think that it was because of either the air or the water in the Rush area that this project unearthed such a huge volume of fantastic work by our local women, men and our youth, forcing the committee to select only a limited amount as they had only a definitive pot of funds to work with. Now that it has been completed it will give all who have an interest the opportunity to dip into this body of work and savour the fine compositions by their peers. You can call into the Library and discover more about your local musical heritage whether it's a song called "Rachel the Ruby from Rush", "The Cairn at Knockabawn" hornpipe or "The Old Mill Bar Reel".

Whatever your preference, there is something in this collection for all to enjoy.

Jimmy Archer

President, Rinceoil Fingal 2021

Ceol an tSraidbhaile Ros Eó

A collection of local
Traditional Irish Music
and Songs from
Rush, Co. Dublin

By Rinceoil Fingal

x

Pat Burke

Pat Burke has lived in Rush since 1996 and has been a guitar tutor and active member with Rinceoil Fingal for several years.

The air, titled "Maureen's Bell" is named after Maureen Stapleton who lived in Rush for most of her adult life and was a close friend of the Fynes family (Pat's wife is Trish Fynes). Maureen was very active in Rush Golf club serving as Lady Captain in 1966 and Club President in 2007. The bell in the title refers to a small crystal bell given to Pat and Trish by Maureen as a wedding gift. Maureen passed away in 2018 and the bell is a cherished family reminder of her long friendship.

Maureen's Bell

Patrick Burke, Air

The march tune, titled "The MV Shamrock" celebrates a forty-five-foot wooden hulled ferry boat servicing Lambay Island since the 1960's. Built in 1962 at Tyrrell's Boat yard of Arklow. The boat used by previous owners of the island, the aristocratic Talbot family in the 19th century, was named "Shamrock". Current owners, the Baring banking family had a "Shamrock" as far back as 1905 and so a long tradition is continued to this day. When not in use, the "Shamrock" can be found berthed at Rogerstown Pier in Rush.

The MV Shamrock

Patrick Burke, March

Richard Clare & Tommy Walsh

Richard and Tommy are two well-known locals in Rush whose local watering hole was the Old Mill Bar on the Old Road in Rush, Probably one of the oldest pubs in the town.

Richard and Tommy, for a bit of fun, sat down one night some years ago and started to write about the various characters and the "carry on" of the regulars who frequented the bar. Once started it grew legs and evolved into an epic poem locally, causing some of the other regulars of the Old Mill Bar to complain that they did not get a mention. Such is the popularity of the piece.

Sadly, all the local characters mentioned throughout the missive are now deceased including co-author Tommy Walsh which makes this poem all the more nostalgic.

Richard Clare and Jody Doolan

Tommy Walsh

Richard, as the last man standing, very ably recorded the piece for us in one take with Jody Doolan on Cello and Valerie Croghan on Accordion providing some background music.

Memories of the Old Mill Bar

In the North County Dublin there stood a wee pub
Where most of the locals were good at the rub
Behind the bar stood a man called Big John
As Taylor found on the night he took him on

Now Maur as you know was a right so and so
As Whelan would tell you in words soft and low
Mickey Condron walked in with a fag in his mouth
And called to Big John for a nice pint of stout

Christy O'Neill in his farmers attire
Sat sipping a pint next to the fire
He let out a roar at Sohrab who had just walked in
'What are you having' Sohrab said 'A Gin'

Dick McCann in his bib and Brace
Sat himself down in his usual place
His brother John who like the odd jar
Positioned himself at the end of the bar.

There sat in the corner a man call P Thorne
Who was wishing to God that he never was born
For he put Rush in darkness one wintery night
When he knocked down a pole and put out every light.

Just as the clock struck nine on the dot
Who should appear but the bold Harry Knott
Dickser was there with brother Mick Toole
Johnny Kelly then arrived, he was nobodys fool

The highwater man was next on the scene
Was none other than Carthy with Big Willie Green
Taylor stood up with rage on his face
And threw out a challenge to the whole human race

Whelan replied saying 'what do you mean'
'Begorra' said Carthy 'watch Will Green'
Matty Sweeney was there with his neighbour Dick Clare
Connelly was restocking, the shelves were gone bare.

Paddy savage sat back watching T.V.
With Paddy Farrell, Jim Fagan, Andy carrick and T.
T'was a Saturday night, the lads were out for a skite
Up jumped Owney Bentley and said 'its a fright'.

In through the door came a man Charlie Walsh
In disguise with thunder and lightning in his eyes
'My Christ' said Thorne 'that man wants lives
Let me be hidden where I cannot be seen
For that man is tougher than big Willie Green'.

Noel Hogan and Sailor wanted a song
Joe Fitzgerald looking around said 'it won't be long'
Just as the words were out of Joe's mouth
Micky Condron capsized a full pint of stout

Joe Plunkett stood up in his new pair of Brogues
The song that he sang us was Boolavogue
Larry Wade not to be out done
Gave us the Black and Tan Gun

With great applause the likes never seen
He diverted his attention to the forty shades of green
The singsong was in full flow and most had a go
The next was Bottles with Poor Old Joe.

Bill Cashe stood up with a full glass of rum
And gave us his favourite The Railroad Bum
We were pleading with Owney for a song all night
But for some reason Owney wouldn't bite.

Just as John Connolly wiped the sweat from his brow
Owney then sang The Sweet Brown Now
He was by far the best singer of all
Probably the best in all of Fingal

They asked Dick McCann to sing The Red Flag
He duly obliged with his own rendition
For truly at heart
He was a real politician.

Pat Monks was conversing with Liam McGee
Pat married a lovely lady from the banks of the Lee.
The next man in with accordion in hand
Was big Joe Lowndes and he took command.

He played a few tunes while tapping the floor
Sea faring Bill Weldon danced to the beat
For such a big man he was quite light on his feet
It was getting late, there was time for no more
John said 'time gents' and we headed for the door
Sadly they are now all gone
But their memory lives on
It was a pleasure to have known them all
The turf burns bright on that memorable night
In that little thatch pub in Rush by the sea.

Written by: Richard Clare
             Tommy Walsh

Valerie Croghan

Valerie plays and teaches the piano accordion with Rinceoil Fingal in Rush. She started learning at the age of 12 when her parents bought her a Hohner 72 bass instrument from the Cavendish Store, Dublin which she still has and treasures to this day. Her first teachers were Johnny Mitchell and Charlie Duffy in Finglas.

They, along with her parents influenced her greatly developing in Val a lifelong love and passion for music and accordion playing.

Val became a member of the WFTA Accordion Band and Greta Byrne School of Irish Dancing in Finglas where she grew up and took part in many competitions and Feiseanna. The Band performed at concerts, parades and festivals in Dublin and around Ireland.

Later Val went on to learn the guitar under the guidance of tutor Karl Alfred in Rathmines and enjoyed playing and singing folk, ballad and traditional songs.

When Val moved from Swords to Rush with her husband and 3 children she joined the Rush Musical Society and for 5 years participated in many shows. It was when Rinceoil Fingal was formed over 25 years ago that Val's passion and enthusiasm for Irish Music was reignited.

A committee was established, the membership grew and it wasn't long before the Rinceoil Band was formed with Val becoming a core player with her accordion performing at various events both at home and abroad. A highlight for Val was their trip to Canada in 2005.

Jimmy Archer

"**Jimmy Archer's Return**"

The inspiration for writing her tune came with a good friend in mind. Jimmy Archer is the President and Stalwart of Rinceoil Fingal and a founding member. When he left Rush to live in Cavan a few years ago he was very much missed by all but his interest, encouragement, enthusiasm and support to the committee of Rinceoil Fingal never faded. He continues today to be a great support. Her tune is a celebration of Jimmy's return from Cavan to live in Rush. She is accompanied by her daughter Michelle Croghan on fiddle and granddaughter Kirsty Burns on whistle.

Jimmy Archer's Return

Valerie Croghan, Air/Slow Jig

Carl Jones

Carl Jones, a native of Rush has been a visual artist for most of his life.

He worked as a background artist and Art Director for over 20 years in the animation industry and spent 10 of those at the Walt Disney Feature Animation Studios in Los Angeles. Coming home to Rush in 2004 he returned to painting landscapes and portraits in oils.

In 2014 Carl signed up for a beginners' course in Fiddle with Rinceoil Fingal. Later he taught himself Harmonica and Mandolin.

Having discovered a new love for music he started to compose tunes of his own. A music he feels comes from the same place as his paintings.

A small selection of Carl's tunes are included in this volume. He names his tunes after his friends and colleagues and his local surroundings. For example "the Walls of Trim" is in honour of his friend Ned Wall who is originally from Trim, Co. Meath. "Ruby's Hornpipe" is named after Carl's beloved cat Ruby. "Tayleurs Rest" refers to the wreck of the ship that sank off Lambay Island in the 19th century. Carls tunes have become set pieces for the Rinceoil Fingal Band with many more new compositions to come.....

Carl's Polka

Carl Jones, Polka

Meeting at the Corner

Carl Jones, March

Tayleur's Rest

Carl Jones, Jig

Steve McCann

Ruby's Hornpipe

Carl Jones, Hornpipe

Ruby the Cat

Triple Note Tune

Carl Jones, March

The Walls of Trim

Carl Jones, Jig

Terry Kirk

Terry is an acclaimed traditional Irish Musician, not just in Rush, but is well known throughout the Country. He comes from a local musical family and started his own musical journey at the age of 12 playing Harmonica. Over the years he progressed to the Mandolin, Banjo, Fiddle etc. to become a very highly regarded multi-instrumentalist. Those who inspired and influenced Terry include John Garry (R.I. P.) who played Banjo, Fiddle, Guitar, and sang. His local influencers were Martin Quinn who plays Accordion, Banjo and Fiddle, and is now the well-known maker of Quinn Accordions. Triona Tammemagi and her Donegal style of Fiddle playing.

He travels to festivals around the country to meet up and play with other musicians while playing regular sessions locally in Rush, Skerries and Man-O-War. Up until the Covid -19 lock downs in 2020 Terry could be found playing at the weekly session on Thursday night in Martins Bar in Rush which was previously named The Old Mill Bar. Most of Terry's compositions come into his head while he is practicing at home. All the tunes are written within half an hour, he claims that "If it doesn't happen within that time, it's not going to happen". He has built up a tidy collection of his own tunes which he mostly names after family, friends and pets. He has submitted 6 of his own tunes to this collection and is accompanied on his recordings by Ray Lawlor and Kevin Gielty.

Discovered in an old edition of Irelands Own is a song called **Bonnie Mary From Rush,** no music or details of its composer were mentioned so Terry kindly composed some music for the lyrics and Enda Weldon sings this version of the song accompanied by Terry and Gary Weldon.

Bonnie Mary from Rush
Terry Kirk/Enda Weldon

Verse

```
C        F           C  F           G  F     C
Oh, Mary, dear Mary, She caught me unwary
    G    Em         F   G  F      G      C
The truth I must tell, she has bewitched me
C           F          C      F      G     C
Her smile is so sweet, and her laughter so gay
G    Em             F      G        F  G  C
And her blue eyes are softer that the moon o'er Lambay
```

Chorus

```
C              F G C                 F    C
She's so comely and lush, bonnie Mary from Rush
    F        C     C G         C
That beautiful village beside the blue sea.
```

Verse

Her cheeks are like roses and her neck like fresh snow
And the sheen of her hair like the evenings suns glow
To none other such beauty the Gods ever gave
Her pure heart is softer than the foam on the wave

Chorus

She wears no rich jewels, no rubies or rings
Yet her queenly walk tells you, she's descended from Kings.
Her form is so elegant, stately and fine
That deep in my heart I wish she was mine.

Chorus

If she'd grant just one smile, or one love look at me,
Like the bard of the highlands, I would cheerfully dee.
Last Sunday I met her on the silver grey beach
She smiled when she saw me, the dear little peach.

Chorus

Oh, Mary, my darling, though your beauty so rare
I must now sing the praises of others so fair.
There are nice girls a-plenty with lips like red berries
They are met anywhere from Portmarnock to Skerries.

Chorus

If you're single in life and need a fair bride
Don't go a step further than old Malahide.
If you're walking for pleasure from Howth to Ashbourne
You'll meet coy little strollers at each crossroad and turn.

Chorus

Oh, I wish I was gifted with sweet sounding words
To do justice to the charms of the lasses from Swords.
And I hope I'll get pardon for leaving so late
To sing of the beauties of dear Donabate

Chorus

If you travel from Kerry all the way to Lough Dan
You won't meet fairer than the belles of Portrane.
I you need a cure for the blues, depression or sorrow,
Take a stroll in the moonlight with a lass from the Burrow.
With the waves starting whispering and dancing with glee
No secret I'm telling you she will comfort thee
She is comely and lush as that heartbreak from Rush
That beautiful village beside the blue Sea..........

Antonio's Jig
No. 26

Terry Kirk, Jig

Kevin Gielty's Favourite

Terry Kirk, Jig

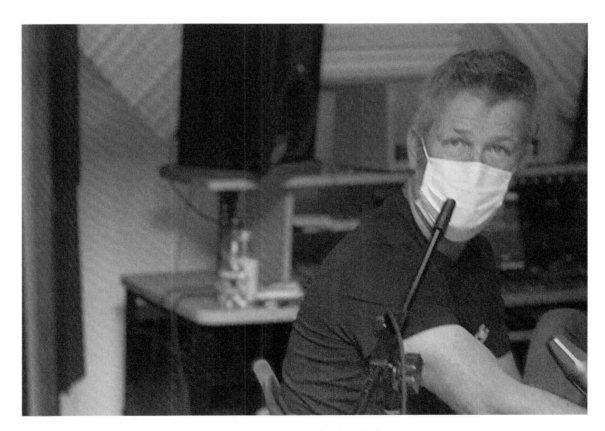

Kevin Gielty

Áine Cantwell's Trip to Lambay

Terry Kirk, Air/Waltz

Sylvia's Jig

Terry Kirk, Jig

Terry Kirk and Enda Weldon

The Old Mill Bar
Terry's Reel No.1

Terry Kirk, Reel

Yvonne's Jig

Terry Kirk, Jig

Chris Langan

Chris Langan was born in Rush in 1915, to parents whose families were native to the area for several generations as local blacksmiths and sailors. His Father David and Uncle James both "Smithies" were members of the Thomas Ashe fife and drum band. His Grandfather, Christopher McCann was a Sea Captain who instilled a love of the sea in the young Chris, who grew up to be a fine boat builder in his spare time and became a founder member of Rush Sailing Club.

Although the Irish language was not taught in the schools during the 1920's, Chris, as a teenager spent time in Connemara living with fluent Irish speakers. He returned to Connemara regularly until he too became a fluent Irish speaker. As a child he played the tin whistle, then at 16 started playing the bag pipes with the local St. Maurs Pipe band, moving on to learn the Uilleann Pipes. By the early 1950's Chris, then married with 3 children, emigrated to Canada to seek a better life for his family.

In Canada, he founded and led the Toronto Gaelic Pipe Band and the Glenmor Pipe Band. He was a founder member of the 1st Branch of Comhaltas Ceoltori Eireann in Toronto. He taught many students the Uillean pipes and whistle and then started to build and makes sets of Uilleann Pipes for his students and anyone he felt was interested in learning the pipes. He then progressed to composing and arranging his own pieces of Irish music.

After his retirement his home became a focal point for musicians who would gather to play or learn Irish music and of course drink tea. He travelled home to Rush each

Summer until his death, to spend 3 months with family and he became a regular at the Pipers Club in Henrietta St. every Tuesday night. He was also a regular tutor at the Willie Clancy Summer School in Milltown Malbay, Co. Clare. He was made a Patron of the Pipers Club in 1991.

He passed away in 1992 but his contribution to Irish music is celebrated each year with the Chris Langan Weekend of Irish music in Toronto and the Scoil Samhraidh Chris Langan in Rush.

Many of Chris's tunes are named after his hometown of Rush, e.g. The South Strand, The Rush Reel, The lament for the Yew trees (written in protest at the felling of the yew trees in Kenure Park), and many more. We only include 6 of his tunes in this collection and thank his daughter Peggy Gibbs for her kind permission to record and publish his works

The Rush Reel

Chris Langan, Reel, 1989

Jack McGuinness

Seán MacAonghusa

Chris Langan, Slow March, 1970

The Sandy Lane

Chris Langan, Reel

The South Strand

Chris Langan, Hornpipe or Reel, 1986

Loughshinny

Lug Sionnaig

Chris Langan, Hornpipe, 1990

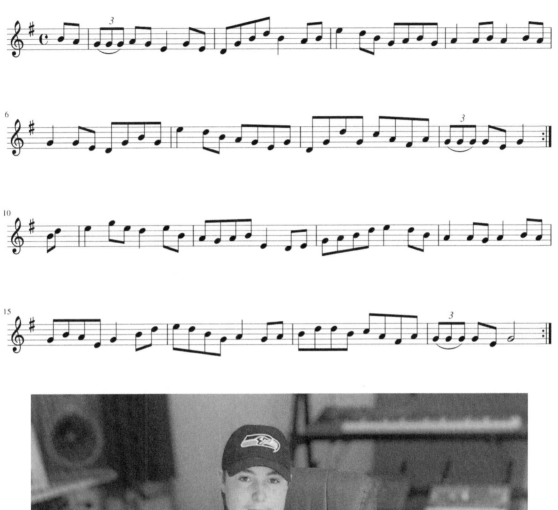

Joe Nugent

Liz Seaver and Jody Doolan

The Lament for the Yew Trees

Chris Langan, Air,1989-1990

Aido Lawlor

Aido Lawlor is a well-known singer, songwriter and guitarist who grew up in Rush and now lives in Skerries. Growing up in a musical family he got his early schooling as a drummer in the Black Raven Pipe Band in Lusk. The history and heritage of the band, along with an early immersion into the Fingal traditional music scene gave him a keen interest in the culture and heritage of traditional music. As a member of the group Dubh Linn, which currently comprises Aido, his wife Helen (Lyons) Lawlor, Ray Lawlor and Fionnuala Lawlor, he has performed extensively at various international festivals. Aido specialises in writing songs in the traditional/folk style and has written numerous songs based on the history and folklore of Fingal including "Eleanor Ambrose" which was recorded by Aoife Scott on her debut album "Carry the Day". He performs another of his songs "Morecambe Bay" on the debut album of traditional group The Bonnymen. He also recorded the album "The Setting Sun" with Denis Collins, the Kerry flute player who lives in Donabate.

Helen Lyons Lawlor

Aido's Songs:

Harbour Wall: (music and lyrics: Aido lawlor)

Aido found this tale in a collection of stories about the history of Kenure House. It describes a campaign by local fishermen in 1505 to encourage the Earl of Ormond to build a harbour wall in Rush – a plea that went ignored for over 100 years.

Rush Harbour by Peter Davis

Harbour Wall – February 2012

In the fishing town of Rush, in 15 and 05,
Too many of our fishermen are no longer alive,
For they work the stormy see, but have no sheltered quay,
To bring them back home safely, so I give to you this plea..

Chorus:

Open the purse strings of Whitehall, Save the Fishers of Fingal,
Come now Earl of Ormonde and listen to our call
Open the purse strings of Whitehall, Save the Fishers of Fingal
C'mon now Earl of Ormonde, Build us our harbour wall

You know your town of Rush, it has fallen in decay,
Despite of the high taxes, that you force us for to pay,
You tax those who work the land, and those men who take to sea,
But a crop that's never watered will no longer be.

Chorus:

Oh you fishermen of Rush, stand up and be brave,
Or else those cruel bastards they will have you in your grave
For they devour the fish we're catchin, and get merry on their taxin,
And not a damn does one of them give about our harbour wall.

Chorus:

Oh there was a good man died, for each one that did survive,
Whilst the Ormonds in Kilkenny passed their event filled lives.
We never got that harbour wall for 100 years or more,
Throughout all of that century the Stormy sea did roar

The North Beach in Rush (music and lyrics: Aido Lawlor)
Aido is very fortunate to have a painting from his cousin and fellow Rush man Paul Kelly, one of Irelands leading Artists. The painting is a particularly beautiful capture of a lady at the harbour wall looking over a scene at the North Beach. The song is a verbal and musical articulation of the painting.

The North Beach in Rush – *2009*

It's a beautiful scene, pleasant and serene,
The north beach on a summer's day
The cloud retreats away, reveals a bright new day,
Blue sky above that soft mist, rush sea has always worn

Chorus:
All through the eyes of one who can truly see,
the north beach in Rush as it is meant to be
A scene summarised, and caught down to a tea,
The North beach, as it is meant to be

From the harbour wall, the cliffs are not so tall
But they do creep up beneath the Martello tower
The family on the shore, they've been there before
As has the lady who can see all in full flower

Chorus:
I step out of a daze, as a lifting haze
Reveals a vision that immediately enthralls.
It hangs above the mantel piece, proudly on the wall,
To be admired by friends and family one and all

The Roman: (music and lyrics: Aido Lawlor)

There are several statues on Rush Main Street depicting important figures in the history of the Village. One of these, a Roman sailor, relates to the discovery of coins at Drumanagh dating back to Roman times indicating that perhaps the Romans did in fact visit Rush. Aido's song describes the possible visit!

The Roman
Composed by Aido Lawlor

A statue it has been erected, history resurrected,

Of how a man came to be, in rush by the sea,

his story now let's reflect on it

He was of a very fine nature, a gentleman not a dictator

He didn't come here to rob, in fact he left a few bob,

He was a decent ould crater.

Chorus:

He was a Roman, a Roman, a Roman, From Genoa to Australia's Bush

Then one day for some spraoi, he went for to see,

The sweet little town of Rush..

The cause of his trip to our nation, is the subject of some speculation,

Did he stop for a ride, on an oul horse's hide

Or did he stop for some inspiration

Was he dreaming of dining al fresco? But found no chippers, chinese or Tesco

There was no harbour bar, no drop in no spar,

All he could find was potatoes

Chorus

He was an Italian Stallion, Commanded a Gallant Battalion,

Now the poor ould Fingallians, a farming their scallions,

They feared for this valiant Italian.

For upon his arrival in Fingal, to the ladies ould cupid he did call

Now there's many's the baby, of an honourable lady

Doesn't look like he's from Rush at all

Chorus:

Now our Roman we've shown him a new home, on the Main St. in Rush carved out of stone,

He'll forever there stand, with his coins in his hand,

Our own Roman Roman from Rome,

Chorus

The Skerries Seaweed Wars (lyrics: traditional, sourced by Aidan Arnold; music: Aido Lawlor)

The lyrics were written around the late 1800's and sent to Aido by local Historian Aidan Arnold, on request, following a story he published in 2020. Whilst called the Skerries Seaweed Wars it refers to a practise at the time by Rush Farmers who collected seaweed from around Shenick Island in Skerries at low tide, to use as fertiliser. This was outlawed by Lord Hamilton, who owned Shenick, after the farmers refused to pay a tax he imposed per load. The song came about in protest at this.

Skerries Seaweed Wars

Lyrics traditional – _sourced from Aidan Arnold; Music – _Aido Lawlor

'Twas on the tenth of March, Our seeds we all did sow
For a little recreation, To Skerries we did go.
The sea was smiling at our side, Our horses' feet were dry
We demanded them a passage, To us they did deny.
"Pull down this pier, Leave this road clear", The gentle lamb did say
"I fear your deeds are out of date, And I cannot find the key".
Into our work like gallant men, We left it free and wide
And led our horses by the head, To wash them in the tide.
The police ran through Skerries town, At us they took a view.
It's very strange to see them there, With little for to do.
They put on us the handcuffs, When they found the work was done.
What a great mistake they now did make, They did not tie our tongues.
We sang our pleasant little song, And danced the chorus neat,
The Skerries people, they came out, And cheered us on the street.
Rush, Skerries and Balbriggan, Are united brothers three.
We pay our rent and taxes, And live in unity.
But this new camp on Skerries strand, Disturbs our peace of mind
And makes us strong in unity, As long as we're combined.

Edith Lawlor

Edith Lawlor is 10 years old at the time of this publication and has been playing the fiddle under the tutelage of Fidelma O'Brien since she was 4 years old. Coming from a musical family, her older sister Ciannait and mother Fionnuala both play the fiddle while her father Ray plays the button accordion. Her mother, father and sister along with her uncle Aido and aunty Helen all feature on this recording. Edith composed her first two tunes "Fidelma's Fancy" and "The Bumpy Road to Rush" when she was 6 years old.

The titles of her compositions reflect the influence and importance of family in her music. For example, "Cons Garden" refers to her grandfather Con, "Nana's Pocket Money" refers to her nana Ann, "Grannies Jam" refers to her grandmother Kathleen while "Tommy's Teapot" refers to her grandfather Tommy.

Edith who comes from a long family history of fiddle players stretching from her great grandfather Pat Clarke and grandmother Kathleen from county Cavan loves to play tunes with all her family including her aunty Siobhan who plays the banjo.

Con's Garden

Jig

Edith Lawlor

Edie Lawlor music

Tommy's Teapot

Edith Lawlor, Jig

Granny's Jam

Edith Lawlor, Jig

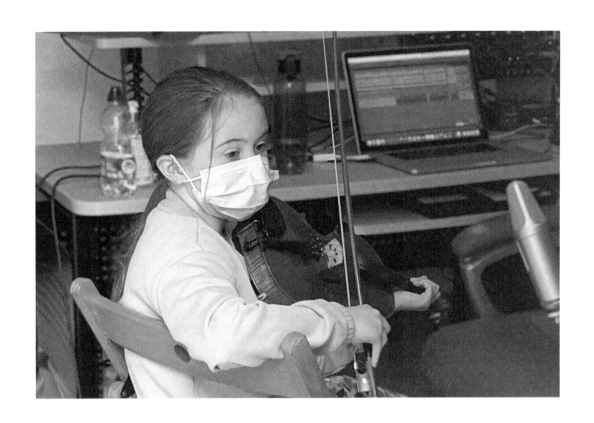

Pat Clarke's Daughter

Edith Lawlor, Jig

Raymond Francis

Edith Lawlor, Reel

The Bumpy Road to Rush

Edith Lawlor, Jig

Fidelma's Fancy

Edith Lawlor, Jig

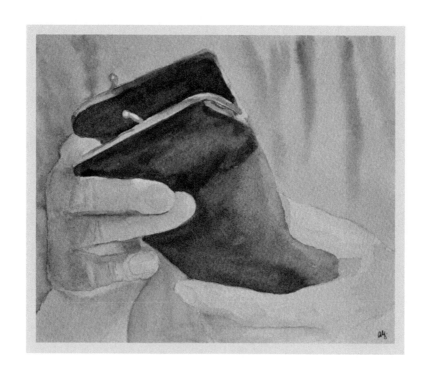

Nana's Pocket Money

Edith Lawlor, Reel

Lenny Martin

Lenny Martin had a lifelong passion for Irish traditional music, culture and heritage Born into a long-established Rush family, he was very proud of his roots and his town. He learned the Tin Whistle under the tutelage of Mary Bergin in Dublin and went on to learn the Uilleann Pipes as a student in the Pipers Club in Henrietta Street, Dublin. His enthusiasm for local history and folklore from an early age never waned throughout his life and whenever the opportunity presented itself, he would champion and promote his hometown and its people.

In the early 1990's Lenny and Jimmy Archer posted a notice locally calling on any interested traditional Irish musicians to meet up to play together. Therein began his journey with Rinceoil Fingal. He began teaching Tin Whistle locally and started many people off on their love affair with Irish music. Lenny became a stalwart of Rinceoil Fingal over the next 20 years never missing an opportunity to promote his organisation and constantly pushed forward with new plans and of course new tunes to learn. Ill health did not deter Lenny from his involvement with Rinceoil and his enthusiasm for Irish music never relented. Lenny sadly passed away in 2018, way too soon, but has left an indelible mark on the traditional Irish scene in Rush and the surrounding areas.

Lenny wrote several pieces of music which are included in this book:

Colette Dowling's Dance: Written in memory of Colette, a young accomplished Irish dancer and musician who fought a valiant battle with Cystic Fibrosis throughout her short life only to be taken at the tender age of 23.

Noelle's Jig: Lenny wrote this piece in honour of Noelle Murtagh, a long standing, valuable member of Rinceoil Fingal Band, committee and good friend to everyone.

 Rush Potatoes, a nod to the farming tradition in Rush, **The Rush Shuffle** an unusual jig and **The Cairn at Knockabawn,** the name of the highest point of nearby Lambay Island.

Colette Dowling's Dance

Lenny Martin, Jig

Grace Moore and Paul Dowling

Collette Dowling

Noelle Murtagh

Noelle's Jig

Lenny Martin, Jig

The Cairn at Knockabawn

Lenny Martin, Hornpipe

Rush Potatoes

Lenny Martin, Jig

Grace Losty and Jack Davis

58

Maire Jones

The Rush Shuffle

Lenny Martin, Jig

Breffni and Marie Armstrong

60

Cyril McGuinness

Cyril was born into a well-known farming family in Rush and from the time he could walk was out and about on the farm. He left the farming tradition behind and set up his own haulage company in the 1990's. He plays guitar and sings so on his long lonely road trips he composes songs, his inspiration being his wife and soul mate Sharon.

God's Plan: Written while driving through a Summer storm at dusk with a beautiful Sky overhead, yet the radio was reporting about people drowning at sea in a desperate bid to escape War and the World did little to help these people.

Gods Plan
Cyril McGuinness

Intro
G Em C D
Verse
G Em C D
I see the storms, A way off far
G Em C D
Raging over the Mountain Tops
G Em C D
With Shards of sunlight piercing through them

Chorus
Am C DScience can explain all of this
Am Em D
Or maybe it's a sign from you
Verse
I see country's going to war
And their people fleeing, with nothing at all
The hunger and death, what's it all for.
Chorus
Lord it's so hard to believe
That evil is out there and it's real
Instrumental
Chorus
Give us a sign today
Lord show us the way.
Verse
They say you walked on every street
They say you healed the sick and weak
They say he gave his life for us
Chorus
So we could all be saved
If we just follow your ways.

Missing you: Yet another song written on the road during a miserable rainy night, wishing he was at home with Sharon, much as he loves the open road, the best feeling is turning off the motorway and heading home.

Missing you
Cyril McGuinness

Verse
G D C Em
If all my life was to fade to gray
G D C Em
I'd pray the lord, for just a day
G D C Em
I'd spend it wise, each breath with you

Chorus
G C G C
Just holding you and loving you
G C G C
Just holding you and loving you

Verse
I'm driving down this Road tonight
Wind and rain would take your life
I wish to god I was at home with you

Chorus

Verse
If I drive all night and tomorrow too
Tomorrow night I'll be home with you
I'm back in your arms, that's where I'll be
Instrumental

Chorus

David O'Connor

David lives in Ballyboughal, a former ESB man, he has also represented Rush as councillor for the Balbriggan electoral area on Fingal County Council for 19 years. Elected as Mayor of Fingal County council in 2015. David was the first non-party councillor to achieve the honour. A long serving member of the Fingal Mummers and keen traditional singer, he has contributed greatly to preserving and recording our local music, culture and heritage.

David has collected and loves to sing old songs that relate to the Fingal/East Meath area. He is a member of the Goilin Singing Club which meet every Friday night in the Teachers Club in Parnell square, Dublin.

He has provided a selection of songs and a recitation from his collection relating to Rush and Loughshinny which we are very happy to include.

A LAY OF LOUGHSHINNY

Diarmuid F.Fitzpatrick

John Dempsey was a citizen
    With energy and push
Who lived 200 years ago
    Halfway twixt here and Rush.
His feet were planted in the soil
    His eyes were on the sea.
And he was dreaming all the while
    Of things he hoped would be.
He thought of Dublin —sorry dump
    Its harbour silt- congested
The dread of every mariner
    Its channel wreck infested.
Dunleary was as yet unbuilt
    And helmsmen were loth
To risk the safety of their craft
    On rocks of pierless Howth.

A picture conjured in his mind
    A harbour deep and wide
With fleets of ships Loughshinny bound
    On each succeeding tide.
The packet boats from Holyhead
    Were plying o'er the seas
And flags of every nation
    Were floating on the breeze.
The agents of the Revenue
    In hiding were at hand
To intercept the fishing folk
    Who smuggled contraband.
As commerce grew and wealth increased
    The village waxed apace
A town became, a city then
    A most important place.
The Lord Lieutenant moved his court
    And soon was imitated
By all the great nobility

All newly decorated.
They talked of moving parliament
    Away from College Green
And putting up the House of Lords
40   Where Dempsey's barn had been.
The Army shifted GHQ
    The Navy moved the fleet
The flowers of fair society
    Abandoned Grafton Street.

45   Ere long there'd be a Woolworth branch
    A "Palm Grove" nice and shady
A fitting background to romance
    For gentleman and lady.
And Burtons wouldn't lag behind
50   with tailoring for men
You don the garments of a Duke
    If you've got two-pounds ten.
"Away with dreaming" Dempsey said
    "I now must realise it.
55   My work alone can that be done
    Or else I should despise it.
As plough that's drawn by double team
    Cuts furrows deep and straight
60   If I'm to cleave a path to fame
    I'll find myself a mate".
A worthy wench he asked to share
    The matrimonial halter
And soon we see the loving pair
65   United at the altar.
John gathers up the ready cash
    Their fortunes great and petty
He buys the tools and hires the men
    And starts to build a jetty.
70   And perch by perch the tide recedes
    By pierhead infiltrated
And in its lee the sea is calm

And angry waves abated.
His wife soon blessed him with an heir
A bouncing baby boy
75   A comfort in his later years
His father's pride and joy.
By adverse fortunes unabashed
Right manfully he toiled
Each year he owned another perch
80   His wife another child.
But children are a hungry tribe
And food, alas, expensive
His bank account began to ebb
As family grew extensive.
85   Then came the day when funds were gone
And work was interrupted
And Dempsey high upon the rocks
By greedy sea bankrupted.
He said he'd see the Government
90   To help him to complete it
He was a man by obstacles
Not easily defeated.

He made his way to College Green
And badgered them till heeded
95   He told them of his future plans
And how much cash he needed.
He made the members nervous
And drove them nigh to tears
Said one "This is the Commons, sir
100   And not the house of Piers".
They said he had their sympathy
His plight evoked their pity
And that his case might be deferred
Appointed a committee.
105   Which worked in Rip Van Winkle style
And duly hibernated
Until the echo of his pleas
Had in their ears abated.

But John was not the quitting kind
  And every second session
He fired his verbal batteries
  To make a fresh impression.
And like a record that's been scratched
  His tale of woe repeated
There was in course of time
  A new committee seated.
They parted with a little cash
  The perches slowly mounted
The family straggled on behind
  A dozen now they counted.
And thus it was for fourteen years
  He battled fortune's tide
And only lost his courage
  When Mrs Dempsey died.
And in a grave at Kenure
  Where sunlight seldom fell
He buried his beloved
  And all his hopes as well.

Eden of the East

Composed by William Matthews (Air – Noreen Ban)

There's a seaside town in Erin that's growing day by day
It's on the Eastern coastline and facing towards Lambay
It's there they grow the best of crops, caulies and the beet
Potatoes, thyme, tomatoes and the best of oats and wheat.

This Eden of the East is Rush where the visitor explores,
It's sixteen miles from Dublin Town and has two golden shores
It's famed for agriculture with improvements up to date
And the finest fleet of modern trucks are parked at market gate.

It is the most progressive town that ever you have seen
With the early crops all sold before, the Sandy Hills are green.
As for every vegetable that ever yet was sold
you'll find it on the land of Rush and you'll find it fairly grown.

The men of rush are big and strong, hard workers to the core
They drive manure from Dublin and the woar from Shennick shore.
The girls they sure are beautiful, they are Ginger, Blonde and Fair
As lovely as the rising sun, like roses in the air.

The young men too are like the girls, they are happy kind and gay
And romance ends with weddings, in the merry month of May
The little boys and girls as home from school they throng
A radiance shines out through their eyes and their laugh rings loud and strong

You should hear the wild birds singing and the pretty pheasants call
Natures music ever ringing and the lark above it all
For verdant trees and evergreens no need to look in vain
You'll find them in their thousands in Kenure Park Demense

There's clubs for boys and there's clubs for girls and sport for one and all
With tennis, football, cricket all at their beck and call
New homes are ever rising mid lovely fields of flowers
The ever-flowing rivers and the old Martello towers

There are modern public services from shops both big and small
To garages and railways, and libraries and all
There's a fishing fleet in the harbour and a coal boat at the pier
And a lovely air from the clear blue, with Howth away at rear.

There's a cinema and dancehall that rise up from the land
They each and all in harmony, with St. Maur's Pipers Band
The sky is roaring blue above, with sunshine all around
And the Holy Roman Catholic Church it dominates the town

There's a growing population and there's bread for those who toil
Some work in the city but most work on the soil
Some have crossed the briney deep to countries of renown
But they ne'er forget old Eireann nor Dublin's Market Town.

Jack Nugent

Fair Maid of Fingal

(Air could be "The Garden Where the Praties Grow (John McCormack))
Composed by Patrick Nicell

It was on a glorious Summer's day all in the month of June
I left my home on pleasure bent upon a Sunday afternoon
For to view the works of nature, when the grandest sight of all
Was the meeting of a fair colleen, the Fair Maid of Fingal.

As I gazed upon this pretty maid I found her sweet and fair
And less than twenty Summers shone on her golden hair
How often in my memory that scene I will recall
When first I met this maiden fair, the Fair Maid of Fingal

Now fair maids I've seen in plenty, yet still none can I see
For charm and grace to take the place of this maid from Ballykea
She is the rose of sweetness, the sweetest flower of all
And sure I declare none can compare to the Fair Maid of Fingal

I've seen the reds and blondies, dark raven locks as well,
Still none like she appeals to me and this to you I tell
She seemed to me an Angel Bright and the model flower of all
None can I trace to take the place of this Fair Maid of Fingal

Fair Maids I've seen in plenty, I meet them every day
With style and grace and smiling face as they come along my way
Still for all their style and beauty I would forsake them all
For this charming little colleen, the Fair Maid of Fingal

Patrick Nicell wrote this poem in admiration of a young Loughshinny Girl. Patrick was born in Loughshinny around the turn of the last century. In the 1960's he sadly lost his life in a tragic accident one evening as he returned to his cottage close to the cliffs of Drumanagh. It seems he missed his footing and fell onto the rocks below. His body was not discovered until the following morning.

Rachel the Ruby of Rush

Attend to my tale each young lover draw near until I do relate
How Cupid the sly little rover he makes me lament my sad fate
A fair one has me captivated whose voice does outrival the thrush
I'm strung to the heart I repeat it for Rachel the Ruby of Rush

It was on a bright summer's morning I walked along the seaside
Bright Phoebus the fields was adorning and Flora displaying her pride
Far down in a sweet pleasant bower convenient to a hazel bush
I chanced to espy pulling flowers young Rachel the Ruby of Rush

I spoke to this matchless Diana come down from Olympus above
Are you the lovely Susanna or Venus the Godess of Love
My fame it got all entangled my heart it received such a crush
I thought I would die I repeat it for Rachel the Ruby of Rush

As soon as my strength I recovered and that my lost speech did return
Some fortitude then I assumed tho' sadly my poor heart did burn
Said I, sweet celestial fair creature I came here my fortune to push
And I count it the grand work of nature to gaze on the Ruby of Rush

Young man then your tongue is deluding to flatter you are inclined
Therefore then leave off your intruding you might as well catch the swift wind
As once for to think for to mock me give over your bantering hush
For all your fine speeches to shock me then said the bright Ruby of Rush

Oh madam I vow I don't flatter I really do speak quite sincere
I don't wish to lie or to chatter I surely the truth do declare
Your angelic frame I admire as you sat beneath the sweet bush
Just cure me is all I require from the brilliant bright Ruby from Rush

Then pray where is your habitation and what is your name and your trade
Or have you got a situation or have you a large fortune made
I wait in suspense for your answer and now it has come to the push
Then don't tell me any romance sir said the Brilliant Ruby of Rush

My love then I hold a large farm convenient to sweet Skerries town
Twill keep us both happy and warm likewise I sell ale that is brown
My name it is Lawrence McNally that soon could a saucy chap crush
And love is the cause of my folly thou bright Ruby of Rush

Then here is my hand I surrender therefore ask my father's consent
I see that you are no pretender when that is obtained I'm content
He'll give you a nice handsome portion if you do the old joker push
Will rise you to fame and promotion then said the Bright Ruby from Rush

Composed by John Sheil (Sheil the Poet) in the 1850's He was from the North and remembered 1798. He moved to Drogheda and is buried in the Chord Rd. Graveyard.

Aine O'Donnell

Aine was born and raised in the harbour area of Rush Co. Dublin and followed in the footsteps of her Grand Uncle Chris Langan to become an accomplished tin whistle player, later taking up the Banjo as well. She learnt her music from Lenny Martin when she was young and spent her youth playing music in pubs, festivals and events with Rinceoil Fingal. She went on to eventually graduate from the University of Limerick with a Bachelors in Irish music and Dance. She was delighted to join this project to honour a town whose beauty has been hard to part from and whose character has been hard to forget. Between the farmers' glasshouses, the back lanes and the views of Lambay from the beaches, this town has always been a place to relax and consolidate for her. So, her tunes were written about the little joys and the community events that she experienced here. From meeting a friend who was perhaps here on a caravanning summer holiday, to seeing the dogs run wildly down on the south beach, to a sombre meeting to say goodbye to a passing loved one (coupled with a few drinks in celebration of their life). Rush was not only the place she was born, but the place that occupies a small portion of her heart, no matter where she is.

Farewell Lullaby

Aine O'Donnell, Waltz

Dogs on the Beach

Aine O'Donnell, Hornpipe

Gary Weldon

Come Sit With Me On The Dunes

Aine O'Donnell, Air/Waltz

Eithne O'Donnell

Eithne's roots are firmly established in Rush with both sides of her family having lived in the town for generations. She derived her love for Irish Music and Culture from her uncle Chris Langan, a piper, who although he had emigrated to Canada in the late 1950's, spent his Summers in Rush after his retirement where he inspired many to take up an instrument and learn Irish Music.

 She has been a member of Rinceoil Fingal since its early days, signing up for the adult whistle class under the tutelage of Lenny Martin in the mid 1990's, serving on its committee while playing the Tin whistle with the band.

"Lenny's thing-a-ma-Jig" Eithne wrote this jig as a tribute to Lenny Martin, who encouraged her back to the tin whistle as an adult many years ago, the start of many happy years of playing and learning.

Kara Nugent-Davis

Lenny's Thing-a-ma-Jig

Eithne O'Donnell, Jig

Michael Redmond

Michael grew up in Walkinstown, Dublin, he moved to Rush in the early 1990's and settled in for the long haul. His career was spent working in the Health Services Sector at home and abroad while he and his family have been active members of several local Sports Clubs. He is an accomplished songwriter who plays guitar and piano. He teamed up with Paul Brennan, another accomplished musician and performer in his own right, to record a number of songs together, one in particular called "Isolation" was released in 2020. Michael joined Rinceoil Fingal in 2019 and regularly attended the weekly band session until the covid-19 restrictions came into effect.

Paul Brennan and Michael Redmond

Having lived in Rush since the early 1990's Michael felt he could drawn on his own experiences to write a song about the town. He wrote the melody first and while writing the lyrics was conscious that Rush has both a rich history and a very active social and sporting community, so he incorporated as many of these elements as possible into his song. He is yet again accompanied by Paul Brennan on the recording.

RUSH

Composed by Michael Redmond

Intro

D D

Verse 1

      D   C
I was young then, younger than now
         G   D
I felt like I'd arrived somehow
    D   A
At the place where I was meant to be
     Em   D
This quiet village beside the sea

Chorus

      C   Em
I was nineteen then, greener than the trees
      C   Em
I noticed the flowers and crops grown in the fields
      F   Em
The waves that lapped against the shore
      F   G A
And sailing boats that tack for home once more

Verse 2

      D   C
Rush was always held in high esteem
      G   D
With it's grand house and gardens green
     D   A
Colonel Palmer and Kenure
   Em   D
And the Tayleur that sank not far off shore

Chorus

Verse 3

D   C
You can see the island of Lambay
G   D
From the links it's just four miles away
D   A
Home to the Barings and the Revelstokes
Em   D
So much history it evokes

Verse 4

D   C
One time there stood an old Windmill
G   D
On it's bank you can see it still
D   A
Music bands and a theatre show
Em   D
A chapel at just a stone's throw

Chorus

Verse 5

D   C
Along the beach you can sit or walk
G   D
On the pitch you can watch or talk
D   A
In the fields you can sow or reap
Em   D
Until it is your time to sleep

Outro

C Em C Em F Em F G A

Notes (Key D)

Verse

F# G A A B A G F# E

E F# G G A G D E F#

D E F# F# G F# E D C#

C# D E E F# E D C# D

Chorus

E E F# G G E E F# G

E E F# G A B B A B

G A A B C C A G

G G F F G A F G

Gavin Weldon

Gavin is one of our younger contributers to this collection being just 16 years old when he wrote "Jack the Batchelor" a lively Hornpipe. He started his musical journey at a young age learning the Bodhran with Rinceoil Fingal before progressing on to learn the Banjo under the tutelage of Sean McElwain. Gavin has a natural musical talent that comes through in his easy-going style of playing. He is yet another member of the Chris Langan family tree, being a grand-nephew. He is currently adding guitar and Drums to his list of musical instruments and he's only just warming up so watch this space.

Jack the Batchelor

Gavin's tune was inspired by a local legendary figure known as Jack the Batchelor. His real name being Jack Connor, a famous smuggler in the 18th century who gained a reputation locally as a Robin Hood figure due to his generosity to the poor. Originally from Wexford Jack spent most of his career as a smuggler living in Rush. His house is still standing on the lower Main Street and is now a restaurant aptly named after Him. He died at the age of 36 in 1772 and is buried in Kenure Cemetery.

Jack the Bachelor's

Gavin Weldon, Hornpipe

Sandy Lane The	Reel	Chris Langan	32
Skerries Seaweed War The	Song	Aido Lawlor	44
South Strand The	Hornpipe	Chris Langan	34
Sylvia's Jig	Jig	Terry Kirk	25
Tayleurs Rest	Jig	Carl Jones	15
Tommy's Teapot	Jig	Edith Lawlor	47
Triple Note Jig	Jig	Carl Jones	17
Walls Of Trim The	Air	Carl Jones	18
Yvonne's Jig	Jig	Terry Kirk	27

Artist Assumpta Glynn

Musicians and Singers

Breffni Armstrong
Marie Armstrong
Pat Burke
Kirsty Burns
Paul Brennan
Richard Clare
Michelle Croghan Brennan
Valerie Croghan
Jack Davis
Jody Doolan
Paul Dowling
Kevin Gielty
Carl Jones
Maire Jones
Terry Kirk
Aido Lawlor
Ciannait Lawlor
Edith Lawlor
Fionnuala Lawlor
Helen (Lyons) Lawlor
Ray Lawlor
Grace Losty
Steve McCann
Sean McElwain
Cyril McGuinness
Grace Moore
Jack Nugent
Joe Nugent
Kara Nugent Davis
David O'Connor
Aine O'Donnell
Eithne O'Donnell
Michael Redmond
Liz Seaver
Enda Weldon
Gary Weldon
Gavin Weldon
Rinceoil Fingal Band

Links to music through ITMA website

https://s3.eu-west-1.amazonaws.com/audio.itma.ie/rinceoil_fingal/A lay of Loughshinny - Composed by Diarmuid F Fitzpatrick 1954.mp3

https://s3.eu-west-1.amazonaws.com/audio.itma.ie/rinceoil_fingal/Aine Cantwell's trip to Lambay - Air - Terry Kirk.mp3

https://s3.eu-west-1.amazonaws.com/audio.itma.ie/rinceoil_fingal/Bonnie Mary From Rush.mp3

https://s3.eu-west-1.amazonaws.com/audio.itma.ie/rinceoil_fingal/Carls Polka - Carl Jones.mp3

https://s3.eu-west-1.amazonaws.com/audio.itma.ie/rinceoil_fingal/Colette Dowling's Dance - jig - Lenny Martin.mp3

https://s3.eu-west-1.amazonaws.com/audio.itma.ie/rinceoil_fingal/Come Sit with me at the Dunes - Waltz - Aine O'Donnell.mp3

https://s3.eu-west-1.amazonaws.com/audio.itma.ie/rinceoil_fingal/Con's Garden & Tommy's Teapot Jigs.mp3

https://s3.eu-west-1.amazonaws.com/audio.itma.ie/rinceoil_fingal/Dog's on the Beach Hornpipe Aine O'Donnell.mp3

https://s3.eu-west-1.amazonaws.com/audio.itma.ie/rinceoil_fingal/Eden of the East composed by William Matthews.mp3

https://s3.eu-west-1.amazonaws.com/audio.itma.ie/rinceoil_fingal/Fair Maid of fingal - Patrick Nicel - performed by Jack Nugent.mp3

https://s3.eu-west-1.amazonaws.com/audio.itma.ie/rinceoil_fingal/Farewell Lullaby.mp3

https://s3.eu-west-1.amazonaws.com/audio.itma.ie/rinceoil_fingal/God's Plan - Cyril McGuinness.mp3

https://s3.eu-west-1.amazonaws.com/audio.itma.ie/rinceoil_fingal/Granny's Jam & Pat Clarke's Daughter Jigs.mp3

https://s3.eu-west-1.amazonaws.com/audio.itma.ie/rinceoil_fingal/Harbour wall - lyrics&music Aido Lawlor.mp3

https://s3.eu-west-1.amazonaws.com/audio.itma.ie/rinceoil_fingal/Jack McGuinness - Slow March - Chris Langan - Performed by Joe Nugent.mp3

https://s3.eu-west-1.amazonaws.com/audio.itma.ie/rinceoil_fingal/Jack the Batchelor_hornpipe Gavin Weldon.mp3

https://s3.eu-west-1.amazonaws.com/audio.itma.ie/rinceoil_fingal/Jimmy Archers Return - Air - Valerie Croghan.mp3

https://s3.eu-west-1.amazonaws.com/audio.itma.ie/rinceoil_fingal/Lenny's thing a ma JIG Eithne O'Donnell.mp3

https://s3.eu-west-1.amazonaws.com/audio.itma.ie/rinceoil_fingal/Loughshinny Horn Pipe - Chris Langan.mp3

https://s3.eu-west-1.amazonaws.com/audio.itma.ie/rinceoil_fingal/Maureen's Bell - Air- Pat Burke.mp3

https://s3.eu-west-1.amazonaws.com/audio.itma.ie/rinceoil_fingal/Meeting on the corner.mp3

https://s3.eu-west-1.amazonaws.com/audio.itma.ie/rinceoil_fingal/Memories of the Old Mill Bar - Richard Clare & Tommy Walsh.mp3

https://s3.eu-west-1.amazonaws.com/audio.itma.ie/rinceoil_fingal/Missing You - Cyril McGuinness.mp3

https://s3.eu-west-1.amazonaws.com/audio.itma.ie/rinceoil_fingal/Nana's Pocket Money & Raymond Francis Reels.mp3

https://s3.eu-west-1.amazonaws.com/audio.itma.ie/rinceoil_fingal/Noelle's Jig.mp3

https://s3.eu-west-1.amazonaws.com/audio.itma.ie/rinceoil_fingal/Rachel the ruby of Rush - Composed by John Shiel.mp3

https://s3.eu-west-1.amazonaws.com/audio.itma.ie/rinceoil_fingal/Ruby's Hornpipe - Carl Jones.mp3

https://s3.eu-west-1.amazonaws.com/audio.itma.ie/rinceoil_fingal/Rush - Song - Michael Redmond.mp3

https://s3.eu-west-1.amazonaws.com/audio.itma.ie/rinceoil_fingal/Rush Potatoes - Jig - Lenny Martin.mp3

https://s3.eu-west-1.amazonaws.com/audio.itma.ie/rinceoil_fingal/Skerries Seaweed wars - lyrics traditional Music Aido Lawlor.mp3

https://s3.eu-west-1.amazonaws.com/audio.itma.ie/rinceoil_fingal/Sylvia's Jig & Kevin Gielty's favourite - Terry Kirk.mp3

https://s3.eu-west-1.amazonaws.com/audio.itma.ie/rinceoil_fingal/Tayleurs Rest - Jig - Carl Jones.mp3

https://s3.eu-west-1.amazonaws.com/audio.itma.ie/rinceoil_fingal/The Bumpy Road to Rush & Fidelmas Fancy jigs.mp3

https://s3.eu-west-1.amazonaws.com/audio.itma.ie/rinceoil_fingal/The Cairn at Knockabawn - Hornpipe - Lenny Martin.mp3

https://s3.eu-west-1.amazonaws.com/audio.itma.ie/rinceoil_fingal/The Lament for the Yew Trees - Chris Langan.mp3

https://s3.eu-west-1.amazonaws.com/audio.itma.ie/rinceoil_fingal/The MV Shamrock - March - Pat Burke.mp3

https://s3.eu-west-1.amazonaws.com/audio.itma.ie/rinceoil_fingal/The North Beach in Rush - lyrics&music Aido Lawlor.mp3

https://s3.eu-west-1.amazonaws.com/audio.itma.ie/rinceoil_fingal/The Old Mill Bar Reel - Terry Kirk.mp3

https://s3.eu-west-1.amazonaws.com/audio.itma.ie/rinceoil_fingal/The Roman - lyrics&music Aido Lawlor.mp3

https://s3.eu-west-1.amazonaws.com/audio.itma.ie/rinceoil_fingal/The Rush Shuffle - Lenny Martin.mp3

https://s3.eu-west-1.amazonaws.com/audio.itma.ie/rinceoil_fingal/The Sandy Lane - Reel - Chris Langan.mp3

https://s3.eu-west-1.amazonaws.com/audio.itma.ie/rinceoil_fingal/The South Strand -Hornpipe - Chris Langan.mp3

https://s3.eu-west-1.amazonaws.com/audio.itma.ie/rinceoil_fingal/The walls of Trim.mp3

https://s3.eu-west-1.amazonaws.com/audio.itma.ie/rinceoil_fingal/Triple Note Jig.mp3

https://s3.eu-west-1.amazonaws.com/audio.itma.ie/rinceoil_fingal/Yvonne's Jig & Antonios Jig - Terry Kirk.mp3

Printed in Great Britain
by Amazon